# KILLER WHALE

## VS.

# GREAT WHITE SHARK

### BY
### JERRY PALLOTTA

### ILLUSTRATED BY
### ROB BOLSTER

## Scholastic Inc.

New York   Toronto   London   Auckland
Sydney   Mexico City   New Delhi   Hong Kong

The publisher would like to thank the following for their
kind permission to use their photographs in this book:

Page 6: © Skulls Unlimited; page 7: © Seapics.com; page 12: © pbpgalleries / Alamy;
page 13: © geckophoto / iStockphoto; page 14: © Brandon Cole; page 15: © Klein-Hubert/KimballSto
page 20: © Alaska Stock LLC / Alamy; page 21: © Brandon Cole

*Thank you to my research assistants, Olivia Packenham and Will Harney.*
*—J.P.*

Text copyright © 2009 by Jerry Pallotta
Illustrations copyright © 2009 by Rob Bolster

ISBN 978-0-545-16075-9

68 67 66 65                                               23

Printed in the U.S.A.              40
This edition first printing, January 2016

Book design by Rob Bolster

What would happen if a killer whale met up with a great white shark? What if they had a fight? Who do you think would win?

# SCIENTIFIC NAME OF KILLER WHALE:
## "ORCINUS ORCA"

Meet the killer whale, also known as an orca. It is a sea mammal. It breathes air through the blowhole on the top its head. Just like you, killer whales have lungs. They hold their breath underwater.

BLOWHOLE

**KILLER WHALE NICKNAMES:**
*BLACKFISH, ORCA, SEAWOLF,*
and
*KILLER OF WHALES*

Meet the great white shark. It's a huge fish that can't survive out of the water. Sharks and other fish don't breathe air. Fish get oxygen from water that flows through their gills.

Like most sharks, the great white has five gill slits.

**GREAT WHITE SHARK NICKNAMES:**
*MAN-EATER, TOMMY, WHITE POINTER,*
and *WHITE DEATH*

The killer whale has a huge jaw full of about fifty teeth. The teeth can be almost four inches long.

Gum line

ACTUAL SIZE

**DID YOU KNOW?**

*If the killer whale loses an adult tooth, it doesn't grow back.*

*A killer whale tooth looks like this!*

A great white shark has a gigantic mouth full of several rows of razor-sharp teeth. It's scary just to look at them.

**DID YOU KNOW?**

*If a shark loses a tooth, another tooth takes its place. During a shark's life, it can lose more than 3,000 teeth.*

**ACTUAL SIZE**

*A great white shark tooth looks like this!*

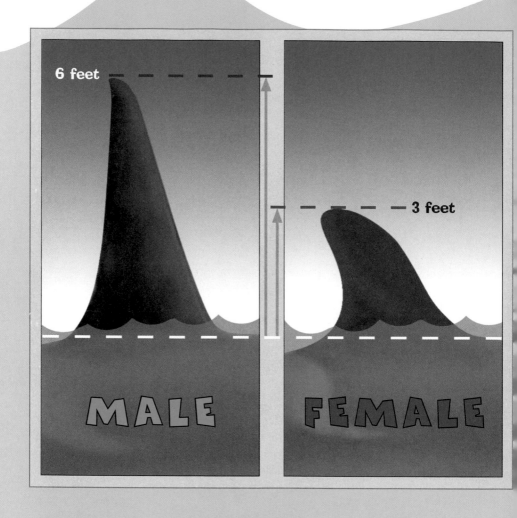

6 feet

3 feet

MALE

FEMALE

The killer whale's dorsal fin looks like these. On a male killer whale, the dorsal fin can be up to six feet tall.

Killer whales can be found in all oceans.

Male and female great white sharks have dorsal fins that look the same.

Great white sharks are also found in all oceans.

Killer whales are meat eaters. Their
favorite foods are seals and sea lions,
but they also eat salmon and other fish.
A killer whale was once seen grabbing a
moose and a deer off the shoreline!

The killer whale is king of the food chain.
It has no natural enemies.

*The ocean is more like a
food <u>web</u> than a food chain.
In the ocean, everything eats almost
everything else.*

Great white sharks eat fish,
but have also been known to eat
seals, sea lions, and even sea turtles.
Now and then, they eat a few people.

A great white shark is also high on the food chain. It is the largest predatory fish.

*Tiny plankton is eaten
by small fish. Small fish get eaten by
bigger fish. Bigger fish get eaten
by larger fish, and so on.*

MALE

23 fee

19 feet

FEMALE

A male killer whale is bigger than a female killer whale
A female is about four feet shorter.

Killer whales have bones. This is a killer whale skeleton

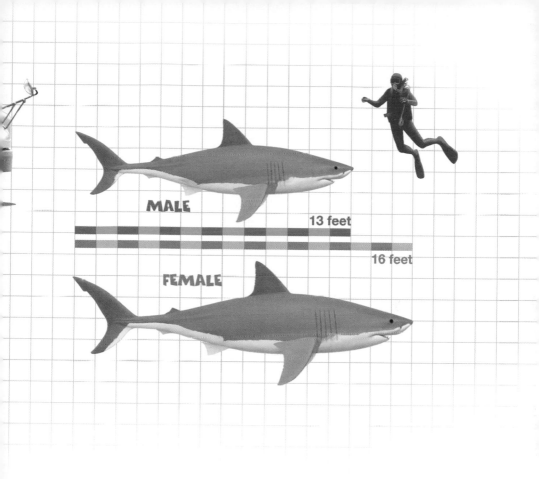

MALE

13 feet

16 feet

FEMALE

The female great white shark is bigger than the male. Females are wider and about three feet longer.

## LOOK! NO BONES!

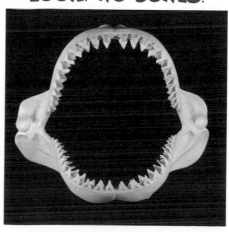

Great white sharks do not have bones. Shark skeletons are made of cartilage. Feel your own ear. It is made of cartilage.

Although they are huge, killer whales can jump completely out of the water.

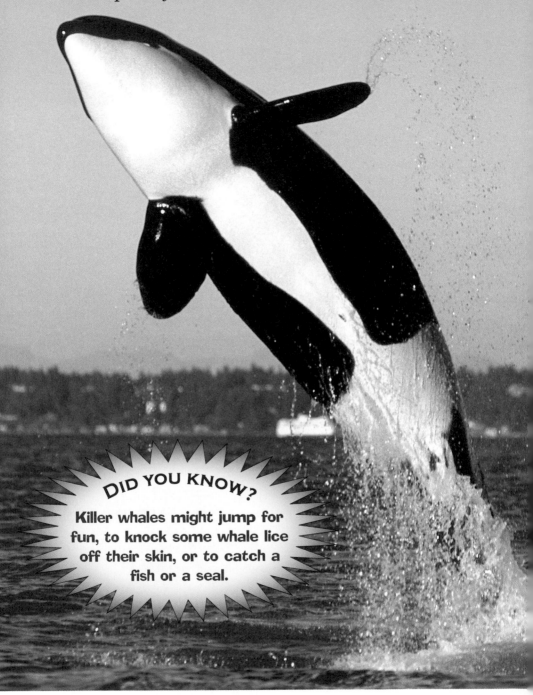

**DID YOU KNOW?**

Killer whales might jump for fun, to knock some whale lice off their skin, or to catch a fish or a seal.

In a fight, who do you think would win? A killer whale o a great white shark?

Wow! Great white sharks can jump completely out of the water too!

So look at the facts! Who do you think has an advantage? Who would win?

Like other sea mammals, killer whales have a horizontal tail.

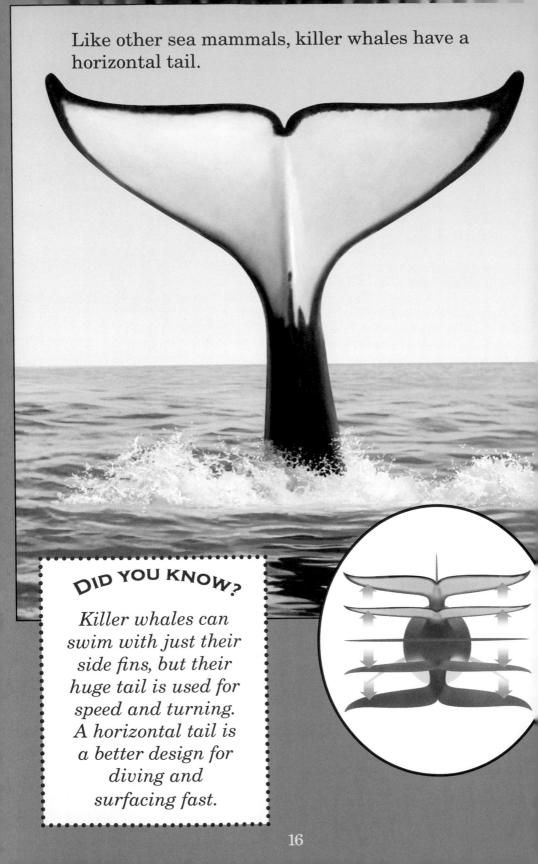

Like other sharks, a great white shark has a vertical tail.

**DID YOU KNOW?**

*Great white sharks and other fish use their tails for speed and steering.*

# SONAR

Killer whales have no ears. They bounce sounds off of approaching fish. They use sonar to navigate, to locate other creatures in the ocean, and to find each other. They recognize echoes and other vibrations in the water. This is called echolocation.

**Bonus Fact!**

## SONAR
**is an acronym:**
**SO**und
**N**avigation
**A**nd
**R**anging

**DID YOU KNOW?**
Submarines also use sonar, but nature had it first.
Bats use sonar too!

*Underwater, you look like this a killer whale.*

# SMELL

*Underwater, the great white shark senses your electricity.*

Great white sharks have a keen sense of smell.
They can also detect the electricity in fish and
other animals. They can tell if you are nervous.

19

Killer whales are family oriented. They live in groups called pods. Killer whale moms, dads, aunts, uncles, cousins, and kids eat, swim, and play together. They look out for each other.

Great white sharks are loners. Two and three have been seen hunting as a team. But mostly they travel, hunt, and eat alone.

Killer whales can stop swimming and tread water in one place. They can swim up to thirty miles per hour. In the ocean, that is fast!

DID YOU KNOW?
Killer whales have smooth skin.

Great white sharks never stop swimming. Seawater must flow through their gills so they can get oxygen. They cruise along at about two miles per hour, but speed up in bursts to twenty miles per hour.

**Bonus Fact!**

*Great white sharks have rough skin. It is like sandpaper. Most fish have scales. Sharks have denticles. Denticles are like little tiny teeth on their skin.*

**CLOSE-UP OF THE DENTICLES ON A GREAT WHITE'S SKIN**

# Killer Whale Brain

A killer whale's brain looks similar to a human brain, but is three times larger. Killer whales are extremely intelligent.

# Human Brain

# Great White Shark Brain

A great white shark does not have a round brain. It has different sections connected together. It is shaped like a letter "Y." Scientists think every section is connected to a different sense.

A killer whale can be captured, live in captivity, and trained to perform tricks. Killer whales are stars at aquariums and amusement parks.

reat white sharks have never been able to survive long
n captivity. Hollywood loves to make movies about them.
reat white sharks are movie stars!

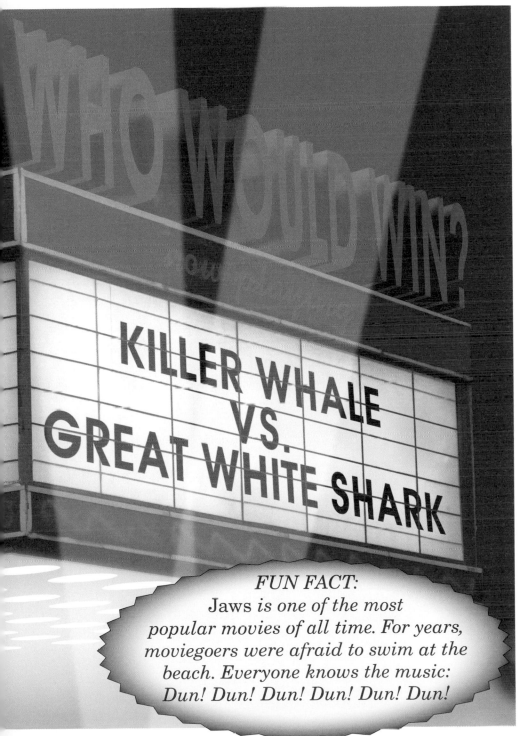

KILLER WHALE
VS.
GREAT WHITE SHARK

FUN FACT:
Jaws *is one of the most
popular movies of all time. For years,
moviegoers were afraid to swim at the
beach. Everyone knows the music:
Dun! Dun! Dun! Dun! Dun! Dun!*

So, what would happen if a killer whale and a great white shark met in the ocean?

What if they were the same size?
What if they were both hungry?
What if they had a fight?

Uh-oh! They are in the same place at the same time! They sense each other. There is intense competition in nature. They are each planning their attacks!

Great white sharks like to attack from below. Killer whales like to attack from any side. They are getting closer. Then the fight happens.

# CRUNCH!

The great white shark makes the first move. It tries to attack with its sharp teeth. The killer whale outsmarts the shark and bites it. One! Two! Three seconds! The fight is over! It is no contest! The ferocious great white shark doesn't know what hit it.

The killer whale won today. What do you think will happen the next time a killer whale meets a great white shark? Who would win? Do you think the shark can overcome a killer whale's superior intelligence?

# WHO HAS THE ADVANTAGE?
## CHECKLIST

### KILLER WHALE

### GREAT WHITE SHARK

| ☐ | Breathing | ☐ |
| ☐ | Teeth | ☐ |
| ☐ | Dorsal fin | ☐ |
| ☐ | Size | ☐ |
| ☐ | Tail | ☐ |
| ☐ | Smell | ☐ |
| ☐ | Vision | ☐ |
| ☐ | Family | ☐ |
| ☐ | Intelligence | ☐ |
| ☐ | Speed | ☐ |